Too Close to Home

Cassie Varyn

BookLeaf Publishing

India | USA | UK

Presentation by *BookLeaf Publishing*

Web: www.bookleafpub.com

E-mail: info@bookleafpub.com

ISBN: 9789360944377

First edition 2024

*I dedicate these words to all human beings,
everywhere. Everyone feels like just pieces
sometimes.*

ACKNOWLEDGEMENT

Thank you to BookLeaf Publishing for creating the opportunity for poets everywhere to bring their own work to life from nothing, and for me to turn my intrusive thoughts in the middle of the night into art that might brighten someone's day.

PREFACE

I wrote this poetry for myself, and for anyone who survived sexual abuse or assault. I don't have it all figured out yet, so there isn't much wisdom to be gained here. But at the very least, you can know that you aren't alone.

This is a collection of poems I wrote, most of which relate to my trauma, and how it followed me throughout my life. It's about learning about this part of me that will always be there, no matter how much I wish it wasn't. It's about how healing doesn't mean the experiences and memories disappear, but that I grow despite them. It's about how much of an imprint abuse and assault has on a human being. At the end of the day, being human saved me. But being human nearly ended me as well.

Never There

Wisps of my hair, you're never there
Move in and out of wishing you were

The corner's dark, the coffees cold
My life's been doomed
since I was ten years old

The fan blades slow, I wait to go
My stomach turns to falling snow

Breath on the floor, nothing to say
Plaster a smile and walk away

With all of the self medication I take
You'd think I'd be better not wasting away
But I still look for you
Every once and again
In the friends lists of friends
In the men I let in

How much can you blame
On mistakes of the past
They keep lasting longer than you
Thought they would last
And sure there was a time

It just didn't seem fair
But now it's so clear that
You were never there

What's there to miss, the rope entwined
Years of being sick and tired of trying

Old cards taped to the new fridge door
Donation bags left on the floor

The question mark of not knowing when
The way you brushed against my hand

Running away and out of breath
Can't help but feel there's not much left

With all of the time I've spent healing myself
You'd think I'd have more than a will to
follow you still
It's the one little message
After all of these years
It's the fray on my jacket
It's the quiet of my tears

It's the way I'd forgive any car for a crash
It's the way I'd take back any sharp pane of glass
Even though I was already cut badly, I swear
I didn't notice before
But you were never there

Sex

Because even when it feels euphoric
And my stars align with his
And the breathing's matched
And our eyes can meet like equals

A smell makes me remember, or
His words are too familiar
Or a touch takes me back there
And the wrong part happens then

The warmth dissipates, just for me
My stars break
into a million sharp shards
that dig their way out
The air leaves my body in a gust that has me
frozen and rigid
And everything tightens
Everything

But he can't find out, even though it's painful
Or he'll know I'm damaged goods
So I pretend it never happened
And close my eyes

Regret

You grabbed your cheeks when you were little,
and looked in the mirror and thought
"I'm ugly"
You said it out loud
That's what gave it power.

You kept saying it
Over and over again
Like a drug
through the years
Rubbing your wrists
Clutching your stomach
Tearing at your thighs
Piercing your skin
Ripping your hair
Starving your body

Why did you have to say it out loud?

Cloudy Memory

There was a sandbox on a cloudy day

Underneath the staircase

I have a feeling that we played there a lot

White paint chipping off the decaying wood

The greenest grass I've ever seen

And pale, pale pink sneakers

Squeaking from wetness, blades of grass
sticking to them

Walking, slowly, up

I could see them between the slats

Every time I see that color pink

I remember that day

The gray sky, and the shoes.

I think it was before I ever felt loneliness.

Living Here 1

Where oh where is the feeling I want
In the sound of leaves hitting leaves
In the coffee just brewed, in the steam
On top of an old book, the dust,
the gleam

They told me I'd find it
Once I got in the stream
And moved with the others
Towards an ocean so deep

But they never said I could get lost in it
And no one told me about the dark

So I stay here now,
in my home on the hard Earth
Looking for feelings
In a sound, in a touch

In a really good show
That I binge watch one night
Eating ice cream with peanut butter
Playing songs from the past

And just trying to dry off from the stream

Living Here 2

The words on these pages say
I need my space
But between the lines it clearly states
Press your face to my face
Grab me close and tangle me up
Don't let me go, or I'll be lost
And spiral downward fast
That's how we live
And pretend the ground isn't quicksand
While we sink slowly
I hope someone will notice
But what if there's no one to grab me

Little blue and green marble
in a big open space
How I wonder
What's the point of this place?

Coming back

When I left him, I left myself

Because so many parts of me

Led back there

So I got a new job

A new hobby

A new home

New friends

New clothes

But by now I've done that so many times

I don't know the way back to ME anymore

Sometimes, I'll hear a song

Or eat a food, or see a person

And remember

I'll grab on tight, then

Piece by piece

I'm finding my way

Giving in to intrusive
thoughts on a jog in winter

Water bleeds into my shoes
And my feet squelch through the mud
I have to get to the middle of that field.
It's completely deserted
And the sky goes on forever
The frost goes right through me
I shiver and keep going, slowly
Breathing out fog
Breathing in ice
Hearing the silence
Crunching the grass
Holding my hair back
from whipping in the wind
I don't know why
I just need to be there,
Right in the middle,
Looking up.

Advice to myself that I never take

Don't breeze by the beautiful sky
Don't breeze by the willow
If days become gravel
under your bare feet
Don't breeze by the pillow

Step on it, dwell on it
Sit down and lay on it
Look at the clouds for real though
Think about what they could be and
could not
Just don't breeze by your free will, so

Dirt

Dirt is the base
Of everything grows
If I'm missing a word
It's all that I know
Too often I fixate
On everything wrong
I could always look up

Could look out the window
Of dead trees gone by
Of mud and the grasses
Of railroad tracks shy
Just shy of the care
That they'd need
To be working again

What's a friend
When there's cold wind
To burn both your cheeks
What's a man
When there's gravel
And chills in your sleep
What separates all
The good feelings from bad

I think it's the deep
It's the truth
It's the sad.

My Greatest Fear, for some reason

Why don't I do what I love for a while

And see what comes from it?

I Still Freeze

I was sexually assaulted at fourteen
In a van
My friends had taken it to a park
To hang out
One of them was a boy
I didn't know
He saw me sitting in there
By myself
He put both hands on the arm rests
Trapping me
I couldn't make eye contact
And I froze
His hand started at my right knee
And slid up
He slowly got closer
As I cried
That seemed to make him
Happier
The more scared and alone
I felt
My friend Lauryn came in
And noticed
She pulled him away
And punched him
She said to me

You have to say no
You have to defend yourself
You have to
You have to
But I still freeze

The Double Standard

My teachers always told my mom
She's smart, but
She is a day dreamer.
She looks out the window.
She stares into space.
She isn't reaching her full potential.
She isn't really trying.
She isn't paying attention.

But in my class there were boys who
masturbated while looking at me,
described how he'd eat my pussy,
fingered me during movie day,
followed me everywhere,
pulled my hair back,
rubbed my shoulders,
touched me, prodded me, groped me,

They never told my mom about that,
Because they weren't paying attention.

Birthday Girl

Lost my mask on the train today.
I told everyone I was celebrating my birthday
with friends.
We would go to the city and dance and eat good
food and be so happy.
The truth is I'm celebrating alone.
When I'm sad,
I feel it deep into my fingertips
That glow and throb with blood
My feet get warm
My cheeks get hot
My brown furrows
But I have to hide it
And hope the mask doesn't break too soon.
No one can know, or my world ends.
Today I lost that mask on the train.

On crying

In school we took a field trip

To a one room school house

We wrapped our sandwiches in wax paper

And tried to be like in the olden days

And a woman, as old as time

Who used to teach there

Spoke to us all, while we sat in the worn,
wooden desks

She said she always looked young

Because every time she cried, she rubbed the
tears all over her face, rubbed them in

To this day, I don't know why she said that

But I always do it.

Finally, Some Solace

After all those years

Of stalling my life

Setting aside time

Going to school

Building my experience

Wracking my brain

Trying to decide on a path

It feels so good to realize

That I could become nothing

And it wouldn't even matter

In the grand scheme of things

In this universe

On this planet

In this country

In this state

In this town

In this apartment

On this couch

Cave

Well I was thinking,

And I decided that I'll stay

Gold smoke in the streets,

And you still tell me about your day

I've read about a million ways to fix my life,

But I still feel buried deep

Just have a couple sandmans,

Tell your thoughts to go away and fall asleep

I've waited,

For too long,

And I'm not strong,

But I'm but I'm not done,

I'm jaded,

With my hair down,

Looking out into the hazy void

Don't you hate it,

All the nothing,

Broken,

Rusting,

Then a hair pull,

And it's something,

It's the pain that brings me out of the deep dark

Cave.

Lucky

I opened the fridge too fast today

A container fell and the lid came off

And blueberries scattered all over the floor

I smiled and thought

How lucky am I

To be able to pick blueberries

In the winter

We'll Never Know

With strangers I'm timid and

Quiet and frail

And I'll do anything that they want

With people I know really well

It's the opposite

I'm actually kind of a cunt

It's this self-fulfilling prophecy

That keeps me from advancing at work

And from maintaining

My social relationships well

Some part of my brain's a real jerk

What taught me to be this way

I really don't know

Was it the holes punched in the wall

Being a passenger in a wreckless car

Being yelled at when the diet coke falls

Or was it the way you'd hug me tight

When you had just come home from a run

And promise me you'd never let anything
happen to me

And I was so scared,

I would wait,

'Til you were done.

Collaboration

Playing music with someone

Connects the deepest parts of our souls

For that moment

But writing music with someone

Makes them forever bound

Feeling Loved

I like to get beaten.

Yes,

Raw and red.
I want purple and blue
On my arms and legs,

To go over my marks with my fingers
Tingle in pain from the touch,
Look at them in the mirror,
And smile.

I want to cry out for mercy,
Wake up sore in the morning,
Stretch up and yawn
and feel...alive.

The pain is a fond reminder,
That someone so recently,
Made me their whole world,
For one little part of time.

www.ingramcontent.com/pod-product-compliance
Lightning Source LLC
LaVergne TN
LVHW010954200726

843509LV00013B/2411